THE D.R.E.A.M SYSTEM

THE D.R.E.A.M SYSTEM

*A **Newly Discovered** Method
to Help You Find Your Life Purpose*

Dr. Carla McArthur

Copyright © 2017 Carla McArthur

Published by Dr. Carla McArther
cmcarthur05@gmail.com

Publishing Consultant:
Professional Woman Publishing, LLC
www.pwnbooks.com

All rights reserved. Without limiting rights under the copyright reserved above. No part of this publication may be reproduced, stored, introduced into a retrieval system, distributed or transmitted in any form or by any means. This includes without limitation photocopying, recording, or other electronic or mechanical methods, without the prior written permission of the publisher except in the case of brief quotations embodied in critical reviews and certain other noncommercial uses permitted by copyright law. The scanning, uploading, and distribution of this document via the internet or via any other means without the permission of the publisher are illegal and are punishable by law. Please purchase only authorized editions and do not participate in or encourage electronic piracy of copyrightable materials.

For permission requests, email @drcmcarthur@gmail.com

ISBN: 978-0-578-19446-2

I dedicate this book to the countless number of individuals who are persistently in pursuit of their life purpose.

Contents

Acknowledgments ix

Welcome xi

Chapter 1   Discover Your Purpose   1

Chapter 2   Relentless Pursuit of Your Goals   13

Chapter 3   Eradicate Landmines   25

Chapter 4   Achieve Maximum Results   37

Chapter 5   Managing Mindset   47

Chapter 6   Using the Keys to Success   57

About the Author   97

Acknowledgments

Special thanks to the following:

To God, for giving me the wisdom and inspiration for writing this book.

My children for the countless enjoyable and entertaining memories some of which I share in this book.

To my older brother Brian, who has challenged me to create my own system, and for our many coaching conversations. His advice has been proven invaluable especially since his first published work was a 600-page book.

Crystal T. for her encouragement and allowing me to call regularly to share excerpts of my book. For listening patiently as I read them with excitement.

A special thanks to Noah B. who made the first investment that contributed to making the publishing of this book possible.

To my friend Traci for providing me a creative space to work.

Welcome

A dream is like a G.P.S. that leads you to success. Without it, you may never reach your destination.

The journey towards fulfilling one's personal dreams can be an amazing adventure filled with enthusiasm and achievements. Whereas, other times setbacks and discouragements become unwelcomed acquaintances on our quest.

But the significance of all these experiences is the knowing that you are in pursuit of your true path or realizing your deepest dreams.

This book is intended to help you attain the life you envisioned by providing you with five essential keys to success.

I learned these fundamental principles in my theological studies while on my personal mission towards discerning my calling. These revelations were incredibly enlightening, and I wanted to present them in a way that everyone can understand them.

Through this book, I plan to support you by conveying the D.R.E.A.M navigation system created to help guide you on your way to living a successful life.

This D.RE.A.M system will reveal the five keys that will do the following:

1. Assist you in discovering or clarifying the journey towards purpose and the life you imagined.
2. Motivate you to set and relentlessly pursue your goals and objectives.
3. Navigate you through the land mines of *Where you are today;*
4. Offer you a plan on how to get you to where you are going.
5. Inspire you to find and manage your resources.

This book is not intended to be a get-rich-quick guide or an overnight life makeover. The pathway to achieving the life you imagine will require time, commitment and determination to go deep within and to take hold of the keys to your success.

The choices each individual makes creates the reality they live. You can decide on the exit you will take on the highway towards your destiny. Each exit you take comes with its own set of possible outcomes.

We all have our own unique assignment that leads us to our passage towards a successful life.

Many people spend their lives defending their life-calling to themselves and to the people who care about them the most. They are left vacillating with uncertainty and are asking these three life-altering questions:

Why am I here?

What is my purpose in life or "IKIGAI: the reason for being?

And, how do I find it?

This book will help you encounter your answers.

Some of you may be living on purpose and need additional support. While others may be living on purpose unintentionally and require certainty.

Meanwhile, some are not sure if they are living on purpose, whereas others feel as though they do not have a purpose at all.

However, all of us have a purpose, and regardless of what category you find yourself in, this book is written for you.

I invite you to join me on a journey towards discovery, transformation and the life you imagined.

We will enter a sphere of battlefields and landmines. Your belief system will be challenged as we uncover some of the oldest and most common threats to success.

My goal is to inspire you to connect to your purpose, encourage you to move away from conventional thinking, and empower you to continue forward towards your life destination.

CHAPTER 1

Discover Your Purpose

Purpose Is Embedded in Our
Dreams, Gifts, and God-Given Desires

Everyone has a purpose. In fact, everyone is born with it. Often, it is embedded in our dreams, gifts, experiences and God-given desires.

What is a purpose?

Purpose according to the Webster's Revised Unabridged Dictionary, is defined as the following:

1. That which a person sets before himself as an object to be reached or accomplished; the end or aims to which the view is directed in any plan, measure, or exertion; view; purpose; design; intention; plan.

2. To set forth; to bring forward

THE D.R.E.A.M SYSTEM

Let me define it in simpler terms:

Purpose means original intent.

- The reason you are alive
- The destiny that began your journey
- Your pathway to destination
- Your roadmap to planning

In Japanese, it is referred to as "IKIGAI", the source of value in one's life or the things that make One's life worthwhile. For instance, one might say: "my children are my ikigai". Secondly, the word is used to refer to mental and spiritual circumstances to which individuals feel that their lives are valuable"[1].

---

[1] Naykiniski, Noriyuki." Age and Ageing." *The Association of Health Management with the Health of Elderly People.* 1991; 28:323-324

How to find one's purpose

You discover purpose by "Living the life that wants to live in you," Parker Palmer.

As a seminary student, I read a book called "*Let Your Life Speak: Listening for the Voice of Vocation*" by Parker Palmer as part of my required reading. Palmer delivered many riveting proclamations.

However, what I found most significant was the notion of letting your life speaks. That concept clarified my understanding of my own purpose and inspired me to embrace the life that wanted to live in and through me.

Surprisingly and unbeknownst to many, our life is constantly speaking.

Unfortunately, many are unaware and deafened by personal, professional and public landmines. How do we begin to hear the direction that our life is trying to guide us towards?

Here are 10 foundational practices representing the starting point of the pursuit.

I highly recommend that you have a journal on hand. *(Note: if you do not have one available, I have included a section for journaling at the end of the book to help you get started).*

Ten foundational practices to help discover your purpose:

1. Submission to God and His Purpose for your life

2. Prayer & Meditation – Ask God to reveal Your Purpose

3. Focus on your deepest, most inner longings. They are the voice of your spirit, calling you to the precise place where you belong. Write them down.

4. Make a list of the following: Current and Past Vocation, Education, Volunteer Work, Religious Activities, Special Skills, Hobbies and other things you enjoy doing. Look for overlapping themes. You can also use your LinkedIn profile if it is all-inclusive. This will give a snapshot of the life that wants to live through you.

5. Write a list of what is most significant to you. Your religious belief? Financial security? What type of legacy do you want to leave when you depart this life? Your true priorities should direct your search for your true calling.

6. What traits do you have?
   (e.g. Adventurous, Helpful, Encouraging)

7. Write down what you are currently dissatisfied with. What would you like to see changed?

8. Consider the needs of your community. How do current needs and opportunity correlate with what you have to offer? Who could benefit from your talents, passions, and abilities?

9. Take a Personality, Career or Spiritual Assessment test.

10. Hire a Transformation Coach or join a group to guide you through the process.

I would like to share a few of our family's twin stories with you to give you an illustration of how your life is speaking through reoccurring themes.

TWIN STORIES

Who Doesn't Want to Save Money?

In first grade, my son's teacher shared a humorous story about my son Andrew who gave her a coupon so she could save money on the purchase of her Thanksgiving Turkey.

Teacher to the class: *"Thanksgiving is coming soon, and she mentions that she will be buying a Turkey."*

The next day in class

Andrew: *"Hi Mrs. Teacher, I brought you this turkey coupon. I bet if you use this, you could save a lot of money."*

Hoagies Anyone?

The twins loved hoagies (another name for a club sandwich on 6-inch Italian bread). The hoagies were freshly made, on freshly baked bread. You could put anything on it that you'd like (… lettuce, tomatoes, pickles). They usually ordered the usual lettuce and tomatoes while I preferred everything on it and with extra mayonnaise.

The best part was the price; the hoagies cost $1.00. Needless to say, that store stayed busy, and my children enjoyed our frequent visits.

One Saturday, the twins spent the day with close family friends and their son. For lunch, she took the boys to their favorite eatery the "Hoagie" store.

After they ordered their hoagies, they paid the owner and left the store.

The conversation shared by Mrs. Linda went like this:

Andrew: (turning towards her) *"Aunt Linda, I bet you can make these."*

Aunt Linda: She replied, *"Yes I probably can."*

Andrew: *"Well, if you make these, we can sell them and make a lot of money."*

Can you hear a common theme?

Snacks for Sale!

I received a call from the twin's counselor asking me to meet with him. He assured me that it wasn't anything serious. The next day, I went to the office. The counselor had this pleasant smile as he shared this story below.

During breakfast, the children are welcome to eat as much as they'd like. The twins would finish their meal and take a few breakfast bars for later. This is fine. Throughout the week a classmate asked Asiel for a breakfast bar and offered to pay $1.00. For several days, the twin's procured as many breakfast bars as they could in the morning to sell in the afternoon.

When I arrived in the office, he called the twins into the meeting. When asked why they were selling the snacks, they innocuously mentioned that students were asking them for the snacks and were willing to pay for the breakfast bars. Next, they stated that they would amass them in the morning and sell them in the afternoon but mostly on the school bus. The counselor explained to them that free meals are free and should not be sold.

Both the counselor and I agreed the twins showed great resourcefulness in meeting supply and demand; however, it was the wrong venue. That weekend I took my children to a Wholesale Club to buy an assortment of candy for them to sell at a local flea market. I wanted them to continue to fulfill their passion for selling and earning a profit by providing them with an appropriate environment.

Thanks Girls for the Donations!

This was an exciting year as the twins' entrepreneurial endeavors continued. They were doing the typical tasks to earn pocket change like shoveling snow, raking leaves, and downloading music and selling the CDs. Nonetheless, the story below is priceless and worth sharing.

Let me preface this story first by sharing one of my child-rearing approaches:

As a parent, broadcast media programming censorship was an important part of my parenting. For seven years we had no access to over–the–air programs. Watching television was rare, but when we did watch TV, we watched home movies.

I replaced television by making available books, board games, and family movies. The indoor activities in addition to the playing outdoors kept them intellectually stimulated, outgoing and physically healthy. Consequently, we had plenty of movie marathons and game nights.

Once again, the twins came up with a new business enterprise. However, this time their new business venture encompassed their sisters' possessions.

The sisters were unknowingly the silent business investors and major contributors.

Over the seven years, one could imagine that we had amassed an extensive library of children and young adult books and had crates of reading materials. Their big idea was the traveling book salesmen. They collected all the previously read books in the house, which included their sisters' books, and began to sell them to anyone in the community that wanted to purchase them.

Naturally, the girls were not happy about the twins selling their books.

The Mary Kay Way… Well, Almost

As a young adult, my family instilled the importance of having multiple streams of income. Subsequently, I decided to invest in Mary Kay and become a Sales Associate. I purchased inventory because I was going make this business work. In my mind, I was going to earn one of those pink Cadillac's or candy apple red Sedans.

Unfortunately, my day job as a senior manager was very demanding. In the evenings, parenting claimed the remainder of my time leaving me deficient in my "time allocation account." Between work and children, who had time for anything else.

You know what that meant?

I wasn't selling any products.

One day I was on a phone call with a friend and expressed my concerns about not having any spare time to sell my cosmetics. One of the twins overheard the conversation and said, "Mom, we can sell them for you." The twins recruited two of their older sisters and went door-to-door in our gated community and sold most of my inventory. I didn't get the pink Cadillac, but my stock was significantly reduced. The twin's entrepreneurial life-force was not driven by lack or greed. It was motivated by the idea that the twins had merchandise that someone else was willing to buy.

Through the illustrations of the 'Twin Stories" we can recognize as early as the age of six, an important application of finances and sales. These noticeable practices and sub-conscious awareness of money matters and sales are a strong display of their assets that will lead them towards their higher purpose.

It is not surprising that the twins would major in business and have chosen careers in the banking and sales industry. The competencies required in their respective industries are proficiencies that are directly connected to their higher calling.

I hope these stories encourage you as you begin to discover your own constant themes and narratives to shed light on your purpose.

How to clarify your purpose

Finding your purpose can be both rewarding and overwhelming at the same time. In many instances, you may experience apprehension because of ambiguity. To clarify your purpose, you will want to make sure it passes what I call the SMEL (Spiritual, Moral-Ethical, and Legal) Test.

Six guiding principles to help with clarity of purpose:

1. Does your mission/ assignment line up with your Values/ Faith/Belief System?

2. Will your purpose benefit others? Remember, what you were born to do is for others. God will never give you an assignment just to make you rich.

3. It will require your dependency on God or a power greater than yourself.

4. It will need the assistance of other people to help you with your purpose.

5. Am I equipped physically, emotional, and mentally for the assignment?

6. Is it breaking any moral or spiritual laws?

Reflection Moment

Everyone was created for a purpose and was given the ability to achieve their mission. Even in our childhood, our lives are speaking. Take a moment and reflect on some of your earliest childhood memories. Can you see times when your life was trying to communicate with you?

Success in accomplishing the life that wants to live through us goes beyond discovery. It requires assurance of purpose, time, and discipline through setting the right goals and the relentless pursuit of them.

CHAPTER 2

Relentless Pursuit of Your Goals

*Realizing Purpose Fuels
the Relentless Pursuit of Your Goals*

Let me start by saying that goal-setting is necessary for achieving anything in life.

Before I discuss the importance of setting goals in this chapter, I would like to share an indispensable secret that I learned. I am disclosing this hidden truth because it is an essential key to every area of your success.

The secret is **EVERYONE SETS GOALS!**

For some readers, this may sound bombastic; however, it was intentional.

While this isn't classified information, far too many people are unsuccessful at achieving their desired aim. This may be the result of the individual's lack of understanding of this succeeding indisputable fact.

Whether we are consciously setting goals or not, we are setting goals daily.

I know this sounds contradictory.

Let me explain it this way.

A person who woke up this morning without clearly defining the goals for the day, has in fact; set the target for the day to be dictated by the occurrence of the day.

If he/she does not set goals to better their personal relationships at best, he/she has positioned the aim for stagnation.

And an individual that fails to establish financial objectives or budget has set a course that will lead to overspending and financial loss.

If he/she continues to live his/her life this way, he/she will have a life cycle of disorder controlled by his undisciplined lifestyle, habits, and his/her environment.

We all had times when we failed to plan, and those were more likely the least productive moments in our life.

What are Goals?

- Goals are the desired result that a person or a system visualizes, plans and commits to accomplish.
- Goals are a fundamental part of a plan that promotes the self-actualization of a purpose.

Many of us are familiar with the **S.M.A.R.T** method. The S.M.A.R.T Formula was initially seen as a business tool.

However, today, it is often used for setting various types of goals.

SMART commonly stands for:

- **S** – Specific (or Significant).
- **M** – Measurable (or Meaningful).
- **A** – Attainable (or Action-Oriented).
- **R** – Relevant (or Rewarding).
- **T** – Time-bound (or Trackable).

Now, goal setting is the process of identifying something that you want to accomplish and establishing measurable goals and timeframes.

Here is a model that I personally like for achieving my long-term goals.

V-I-P-E-R is a 5-step guide, which lists the five crucial steps for successful goal accomplishment.

VIPER is a term that is used for several different things… cars, airplanes, snakes… things with power.

With VIPER, you will discover that it gives you the force to relentlessly pursue goals that appear to be the most challenging to attain.

These five steps are:

- **V** – Visualize: Truly imagine the goal
- **I** – Implement: Implement techniques to succeed in the goal
- **P** – Planning: Distinguish plan factors based on the techniques
- **E** – Execution: Get moving on the plan and goal
- **R** – Recap: Evaluate the outcome and future steps

Align Your Personal Goal with Your Purpose

There are eight different areas highlighted that you will need to focus on when setting your personal goals.

The Wheel of Life

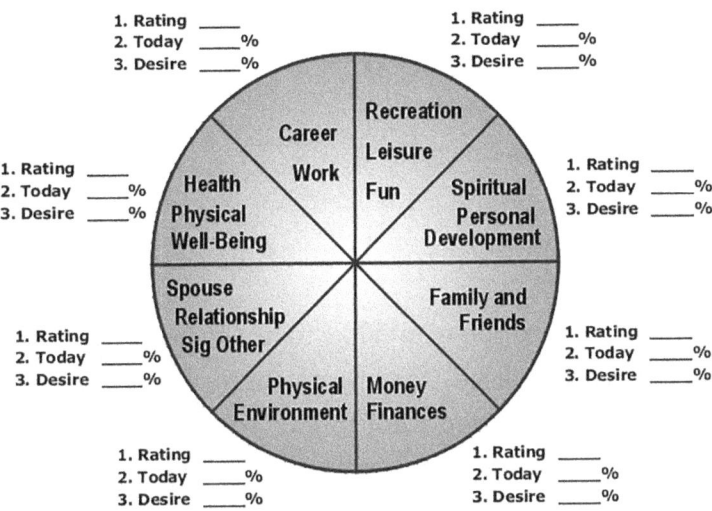

The best approach to goal setting in these areas is to do a self-assessment by applying the following question to each part of the Wheel of Life.

Am I happy with where I am today?

On the scale of 1-5, with one being the "least satisfied" and five "most satisfied."

Spiritual Growth	1	2	3	4	5
Relationships/Marriage	1	2	3	4	5
Finances	1	2	3	4	5
Fun & Recreation	1	2	3	4	5

Health	1	2	3	4	5
Career	1	2	3	4	5
Persoanal Development	1	2	3	4	5
Physcial Environment	1	2	3	4	5

Next, identify where you would like to be (that which you would consider as most satisfied.). Think of your goals as your roadmap for getting you where you want to go.

Next, prioritize your planning based on greatest need and importance.

Note: We will revisit this question along with others in this chapter as we continue.

Remember, if you neglect to give each part the proper attention and maintenance required as you move toward your God-given purpose, you will experience difficulties and lack of balance.

Illustration: Rich Man and Poor Man

Dr. Rich and Mr. Poor are two young men who shared a desire to help others by becoming a doctor. Dr. Rich understood the principles of setting goals and matriculated through college, medical school, and completed a 5-year general and 2- year cardiac residency. Afterward, he passed the Medical Licensing Examination to become a Cardiothoracic Surgeon.

Congratulations Dr. Rich!

For not only setting goals, but also completing them.

Disappointingly, Mr. Poor also knew the benefits of goal setting. However, he chose to awaken each morning and failed to have a plan for his day.

Meanwhile, he enjoyed spending his afternoons drinking beer and watching his favorite television shows.

Moreover, Mr. Poor neglected the benefits of planning for his success and never completed college or fulfilled his dream of becoming a doctor.

Mr. Poor prepared for failure because he failed to plan for his success. Mr. Poor could have changed his outcome by regularly revisiting "the thirteen benefits of goal-setting" listed below.

Thirteen Benefits of Setting Goals

Goal Setting:

1. It is the prerequisite of the ultimate end goal.
2. Provides the structure of your plans.
3. Gives specifics to the plan.
4. Offers a starting and ending point.
5. Delivers growth measures of unlimited progress.
6. Protects us from landmines.
7. Helps you to stay focused.
8. It is the architect of discipline.
9. Generates drive to help you move forward.
10. Holds you accountable.
11. Helps you achieve your highest potential.

12. Offers you the opportunity to live your best life.

13. Success comes from the discipline of goal-setting according to your purpose.

Now that we covered some of the values of goal setting, I would like to share a free tool called Trello that I use regularly.

Trello is a free productivity system that allows you to create boards to organize individual projects.

Some refer to Trello as a Game of Life Board. I prefer to call it a Vision Board because it allows us to bring to life what we envisioned.

One of the great things about Trello is that this platform can be accessed anywhere and used to organize your ideas through the use of boards, cards, pictures, and lists.

Setting Up Your Vision Board

Before creating your Vision Board, there are a few questions that you will need to answer.

1. What do I want to do?

2. Who do I want to be?

3. What do I want to see?

4. Where do I want to go?

THE D.R.E.A.M SYSTEM

5. What do I want to have?

6. Who do I want to spend more time with?

7. What would be the most fun?

8. What is missing in my life?

9. What is stopping me from achieving these goals?

10. What do I want to stop doing?

After, you have answered these questions you are ready to set up your Vision board. Go to *www.trello.com*.

Here is a view of what the board should look like after you add the cards to reflect the questions.

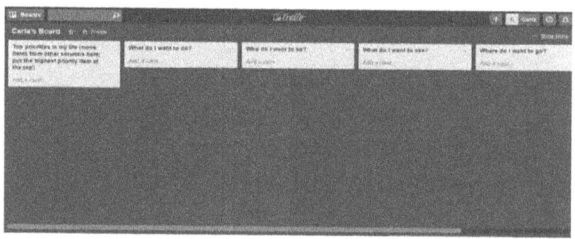

You can also add pictures for visualization. Your board should look like this one, once you add your pictures.

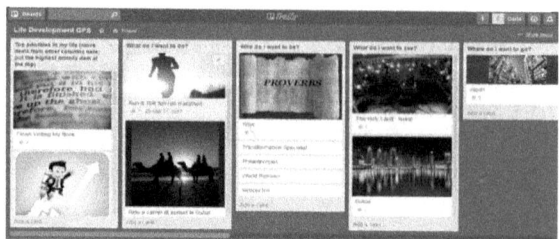

We are just beginning our boards and will come back to your Vision Board in Chapter IV.

Reflection Moment

Our lives depend on the goals we set or neglect to establish. Where we are in life today is as a result of the goals we implement. Are you happy with where you are in life today? If not, make a commitment today to create a new agenda and relentlessly pursue them as though your life depends on it.

CHAPTER 3

Eradicate Landmines

Dream Busters are like landmines, when they explode they have a way of disabling progress

I am sure some of you are asking yourself "*What do landmines have to do with purpose, goals, and plans, or, achieving the Life, Relationships and Business Success I imagined?*"

Others are possibly thinking this sounds as though we are preparing for combat.

As a matter-of-fact, we are!

We are getting ready for the battle to eradicate some of the conscious and unconscious dream-busting traps that block our progress toward success.

My hope is that you will recognize the landmines in your life, break through, and eliminate the traps and barriers in your way by the end of this chapter.

What is a Landmine?

A landmine is a buried explosive device or traps that are hard to see.

I use the word "landmine" metaphorically to characterize the destructive nature of dream busters and hidden traps.

Mines both literally and figuratively remain dangerous long after they have been deployed. Subsequently, creating obstacles and triggering a setback.

Now, that you have an explanation of a landmine in the context of which it is intended.

Let us move forward and identify some of these mines.

Pay close attention to those that you can most identify with.

Two Forms of Landmines

The landmines can be activated in two ways. Psychological Landmine and the other as Physical Landmine.

1. **Psychological/Internal Landmines**

Through this faculty, the mines impact the individual's value system, belief system, emotions, motives, reasoning, or behavior. It is used to invoke one's acknowledgments of or reinforce unfavorable attitudes and behaviors.

2. **Physical/External Landmines**

Through this faculty, the mines impact the individual physically, externally, or tangible. With objects existing in a form that you can be touched or seen.

Types of Dream Busting Landmines

External	Internal
Unfocused	Procrastination
Low Energy	Lack Discipline
Naysayers	Lack Confidence
Stress	Negative Self-Talk

Barriers to Success and How to Break Through Them

It is In Your Hands	Environment barriers can contribute to a lack of success. Here are a few tips to help you overcome them.
Low Energy A feeling of fatigue.	Rule out health problems; Exercise; Shed extra weight; Drink plenty of water; Get enough rest;
Stress **Is A feeling strain or pressure**	Identify the sources of stress in your life Learn healthier ways to cope with stress Connect to others; Make time for fun and recreation.
Naysayers A person who reliably expresses negative and cynical views.	Safeguard your goals from them; Eject them from your life (if you can); Ignore them; Don't tell them what you are doing.

Lack of Focus The act of not having a concentrating interest or activity on some things	Clear the noise; Train your brain to focus; Minimize multitasking; Designate your perfect working spot.
Physical Disability The limitation of a person's physical activity, movement, agility or stamina.	Reflect on the accomplishments of past and present Giants with physical impairments (i.e. Helen Keller, Beethoven, Nicholas James Vujicic, Jessica Cox; Remember, you are created with a purpose.
It is All In Your Head	Mental barriers can contribute to lack of success here are a few tips to help you overcome them.
Negative Self Talk The expression of thoughts or feelings which are counter-productive and have the effect of de-motivating oneself.	Write down all the positive things that people have said to you and read them out loud; Put things in perspective; Read daily affirmations. Use goal-directed thinking; Use positive thinking.
Lack of Confidence Lacking the belief in oneself and their abilities.	Know your strengths and weaknesses; Use criticism as a learning experience; Set a small goal and achieve it;
Lack of Discipline The inability to control and motivate you or stay on track and do what is right.	Prioritize tasks; Dump the excuses; Ignore the naysayers; Create an action plan and follow it; Identify likely obstacles.

Procrastination The inability to control and motivate yourself or stay on track and do what is right.	Get a coach or motivation buddy; Make yourself accountable; Schedule time blocks; Limit your time on social networks unless it is your job. Have some quiet time every day; Promise yourself an award; Make your task meaningful.
Fear Uncertainty & Doubt (FUD) A feeling of insecurity; false information and a display of the appeal to fear; lack of faith.	Bury your fear and acknowledge your talents; Prepare for different possibilities; Focus on what you can control; Know when to trust your instincts; Apply faith.

Naysayers Null and Void

As a young divorced mother of five children, I came to the conclusion that I no longer wanted rent. Rent for larger families was equivalent to paying a mortgage, taxes, and association fees. I also had an unremitting desire to change our lifestyle. I felt the road to economic empowerment and financial freedom included Real Estate.

To accomplish this objective, I used both the SMART and VIPER model for mapping out my plan of action.

Hence, I made a conscious decision to buy a house before the end of the upcoming year. At that time, I was employed in a management position with average compensation that would position me to find a suitable home.

Using the VIPER theory, I started envisioning the style of house I desired to live in and lifestyle ideal for my children. I scheduled private or exclusive showings, viewed at-home magazines, and researched them online.

S – It was more cost effective for me to buy and not rent

M – I wanted to accomplish this within a year.

A – This was attainable because I was employed with a decent income and excellent credit.

R – This was relevant to my wanting to provide a different lifestyle for my family and begin to build a financial portfolio.

T – It was time-based because I gave myself 12 months.

During that time period, I had family members trying to discourage me from purchasing a house. Instead of being enthusiasts, they were landmines. They consistently expressed their negative and cynical opinions about all the difficulties that came with buying a home.

I couldn't cut the family members completely out of my life; therefore, the conversation about house hunting ceased.

The pessimistic exchange from family members went outside our familial environment; it extended to my children's school as well.

Each time my daughter would share her excitement with her teacher about moving and not attending the upcoming school year, the teacher replied in a condescending manner, "You guys aren't going anywhere, and you will be right back here next year."

This was another landmine that we had to ignore to continue moving forward with our plans.

Despite the naysayers and probabilities of failure, I had faith and confidence that I could accomplish this goal as a single mother. I did not want to walk in doubt and fear.

Accordingly, I conducted a research on the subject of *"How to Buy a House"* and developed a plan of action. I stayed focused and followed every step, and within six months I found a house. I made my down payment and needed to come up with the closing cost.

Next, I reviewed my finances with a new goal of attaining the amounted necessary for closing.

During that time, I took pleasure in ordering religious magazines and CDs. I was proud to call myself a card-carrying long- time subscriber. I was buying new books, magazines, and music monthly.

I don't remember the amount I was spending on personal and spiritual development. However, I knew I had to cancel my subscription to meet my financial goal. Moreover, I had enough new reading and listening materials to last another two years.

Afterward, I discontinued the Cable and all other non-essentials that we did not need. Within two months, I was at the closing table and walked away with possession of my keys to our new home.

The Fear of Uncertainty

My governing psychological landmine was fear of change, which stemmed from an earlier experience that went awry. Subsequently, I developed this fear that would inform and influence my personal and professional decisions in areas that I could not conclusively imagine.

Intermittently, making extemporaneous decisions became extremely challenging. Before deciding, research and analysis needed to be conducted before I reached a conclusion or resolution. This certainly sounds reasonable; however, there were times when the situation needed my immediate response.

Several years ago, I worked for an organization that received government contracts. As a senior manager, I made decisions successfully daily. I knew the industry and was more than qualified for the position.

At the end of our contract year, the company needed to put together a Request for Proposal (RFP) as part of the rebidding process. The contract was extremely competitive, as several other companies were bidding on that same contract. I, along with the other senior management team, had to draft the proposal to be presented in Washington, D.C. at the convention.

I was extremely confident with my participation in the development of the RFP because I had a thorough understanding of the organizations, their mission, and our customers. I had successfully managed daily operations of five key areas, six remote locations, and more than 50% of the government contract with fiscal responsibility in the millions.

Once the project was completed, it was suggested that I represent the organization as the presenter. I gracefully declined because of my fear of the unknown. This convention was an unfamiliar environment, and I did not have sufficient information that was necessary for me to accept the endorsement. So, it was decided that the interim Executive Director would be the designated presenter.

Three days before the convention I was on the early flight to DC. I settled in my hotel room and rested for a few hours before the first of many events on the itinerary.

On the day of the presentation, there were more than a thousand attendees. We had representatives from the federal government, executives from several different corporations, contractors, director and managers from other agencies representing the 125 affiliate organizations nationwide including Puerto Rico and the Virgin Islands.

As we were setting up the PowerPoint to present, I was informed that I was going to be the presenter. I had not prepared, rehearsed or reviewed the information since we completed the project. Immediately I expressed my concerns. My concerns were noted but it did not alter the superior's decision.

After the introductions, I delivered what many of my colleagues called an "exceptionally well-done" presentation. My detailed knowledge of the organization and participation in developing the plan was evident and displayed during the presentation. As a result, I received numerous compliments from many of the other contributors.

That day I realized that my fear of the unknown was unwarranted. I was adept at delivering information to large groups, and the annexation of an ignored proficiency emerged. Had I not stepped outside of my comfort zone, I would have missed the field of possibility.

Today, the fear of the unknown intermittently tries to reappear, but I have learned to quickly dismiss the thought and not allow it to have any control over my life.

Reflection Moment

Everyone experiences mental and physical obstacles and setbacks at some point in their lifetime. Undoubtedly, they may even re-appear spasmodically, but you do not have to allow the landmines to stay and take up residence.

Those dream-busters that are the naysayers do not want your dreams to become a reality. **Release Them!**

They do not have your best interest at heart.

Once you serve the mines their eviction notice, do not permit them to return. How you navigate and eliminate them will make the difference between success and failure.

CHAPTER 4

Achieve Maximum Results

Planning purposely, passionately and persistently will often yield the maximum results you envisioned.

Congratulations!

You have navigated through the landmines and made it to this chapter.

Thus far, we have clarified our purpose, set our goals, and removed the mines. Now you may be wondering how I can turn my goals into realities.

The next step is for you to create a development action plan to outline the "HOW" to achieve maximum results that will guide you across the finish line.

Just like your goals, your plan needs to be specific and detailed as possible.

But first, let's look at what a plan is.

What is a plan?

A plan is like a map. It shows the final destination and typically the best way to get there.

Question:

Have you ever experienced being a passenger in a car with someone who refused to use a map or ask for directions?

Well, I certainly have.

And, there is nothing more mind freezing and backside numbing than sitting for hours with someone who does not know how to get us to our destination.

We were definitely lost.

Ok. Maybe not that lost, but you get the point I am making.

There is a simple solution to directionless, and that is to use a roadmap or GPS; more specifically a strategic action planning system.

A plan stops us from living life haphazardly, and we should not live life without one.

Personal Strategic Action Planning

There are several forms of strategic action planning instruments used in various sectors, and they can vary in the number of steps required.

Some are comprehensive and detailed while others are narrower in scope.

Nonetheless, we will focus on a four element Personal Strategic Plan because it pertains precisely to our agenda.

Let's look at Personal Strategic Action Planning.

Personal strategic action planning is a disciplined thought process which produces fundamental decisions and actions that shape and guide your future.

It focuses on who you are, where you are going, what you do, and how, when and why you do it.

Six Benefits of Planning

1. It determines your destiny as seen in the illustration with Dr. Rich and Mr. Poor.

2. It identifies and establishes your goals and what it will take for you to get to your destination.

3. It prioritizes your goals and arranges them in order of priority.

4. It organizes them in steps.

5. It disciplines your life according to your goals.

6. It allows you to see how much you have progressed towards your intended goal and how far you are from your destination.

Knowing where you are is essential for making good decisions on where to go or what to do next.

How to create your action plan

Personal action plans are comprised of four main elements.

1. The first item is a list of the specific steps that must be taken for you to achieve your goals.

2. The second element is the time factor that you use to motivate yourself to achieve the goal on or before a specified date.

3. The third part is listing the resources available to help you realize your goals.

4. The fourth part is to review/ readjust when necessary.

To continue with our next step, we are going to return to our Vision Board that we created in Chapter Two.

Do you have the board set up? If not, do so before continuing.

Great job!

Now let's start prioritizing your dreams.

Here's how:

Step-by-Step Guide for Prioritizing Your Goals in Trello

Arrange the card with your highest priority first, the other cards following consecutively, and ending with the lowest importance at the bottom.

Next, take the top two cards from each category and move them to your first column. Then prioritize this column in the order of highest to the lowest importance as you have done with the previous sections.

Lastly, create a reminder in your calendar to review your Vision Board in six months to ensure your goals are still relevant.

Are you ready to transform your dreams into reality?

Introducing Kanban

The Kanban in Japanese is characteristically translated to mean "card you can see." This concept was created by Taiichi Ohno who is credited with creating the idea while working at Toyota.

A personal Kanban is a productivity system that is easy to get started with, only has two real "rules," and is designed to give you a simple, visual look at what is on your plate, what your priorities are, and what you have accomplished.

Using a Kanban system, you move cards through a board similar to what we just completed in Trello to help you visualize your workflow through different stages of a lifecycle.

Think of Kanban as a system that is superior to the traditional to-do list.

Two Major Personal Kanban "rules"

1. **Visualize Your Work** – You should at any time be able to look at your entire assignment, be able to determine quickly what you should work on next, have visual cues for priority and time to complete, and that system should be easy to add, remove, and reorganize.

2. **Limit Your Work In Progress (WIP)** – restrict the number of things you work on at the same time. This does two things. First, it makes is easier to visualize your work because you control how much activity you have going on at one time.

Secondly, it helps you to stay focused and avoid the dangers of multi-tasking and feeling overwhelmed.

Here is an example of what the Kanban looks like;

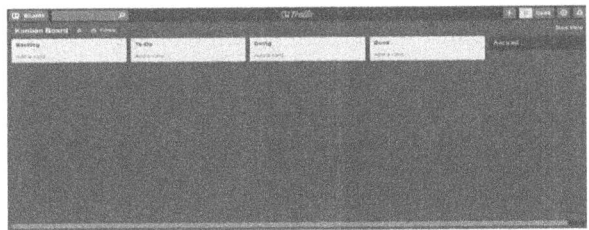

A simple Kanban board includes a chart with four vertical col-umns: Backlog, To-Do, Doing, and Done.

Your **"Backlog"** is all of the to-dos you aren't working on right now, but need to get to at some point.

"To-Do" section is for the important things that you need to do.

Your **"Doing"** section consists of all of the to-dos you're working on right now, or plan to work on immediately.

"Done", this section is for assignments completed. It is important to keep this section on your Kanban; as this will help keep you motivated and productive.

To create this new board: Open Trello.(And create a free account if you haven't already.)

Click "Boards" at the top left of the page.

Click "Create New Board."

For the title, name it Kanban.

I recognize this chapter has a lot of information; if you need to take a break for a few minutes to relax before continuing, I understand.

I had to take a few minutes myself.

Integrating Your Vision Board Into Your Kanban Board

To integrate your boards, you will need to do the following:

- Move the top cards from your Vision Board to your new Kanban.

- Rewrite each card so it is a SMART goal and include the deadlines.

To move the cards from Trello to your Kanban Board

Click the card.

Under "**Action**" click "Move."

Select the "**Kanban**" board and the "Backlog" column.

Repeat for each card in your "**Top priorities in my life**" list.

To add your due dates:

Click the card.

Click "**Due Date.**"

Select **your date.**

Click "**Save.**"

Remember

Step 1: Put everything you think of into your backlog.

Step 2: Prioritize items in your backlog, and move essential items to your "To-Do" column.

Step 3: Move your 2–3 most important items into your "Doing" column – these are an assignment that you are currently doing.

Your Kanban should resemble this.

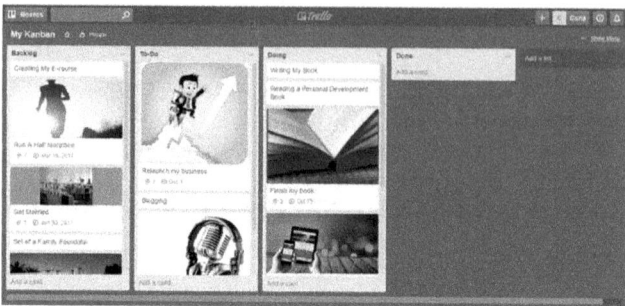

For larger goals create a separate Kanban Board for that particular assignment.

For example: If you have a goal to run a 10k marathon, or to lose 20lbs, etc. Break down all the steps needed to accomplish this aim. Begin with the end in mind and work backwards.

Also, do not forget to view your Kanban daily. I pinned my Kanban to Chrome as a reminder.

Reflection Moment

Remember, to obtain your desired results, you must be purposeful and persistent as lack of planning leads to unpredictable outcomes. Plans may change, but your destination is permanent when you encounter unforeseen detours. Regulating time and change are key elements to achieving maximum results and an essential ingredient in the recipe for success. Use Trello and Kanban as suggested or your favorite management tool to help.

CHAPTER 5

Managing Mindset

*Management of life's resources effectively
is principal to progress*

Did you know that managing of your life resources effectively is a principle to development?

What are life's resources?

How does this integrate with my purpose?

All these questions will be addressed in this chapter; but first, let's define management and mindset separately.

Management can be defined as the practical use and efficient application of resources.

While Mindset is simply the traditional set of attitudes you hold.

A management mindset is not exclusive to the business environment anymore.

In fact, I would declare that a managing mindset is personal and should be a vital part of every aspect of our life.

Why?

Well, it is because a managing mindset sees an investment opportunity in maximizing their resources to get the most value or best return on their asset.

Before we can get the most out of our resources, we will have to pinpoint what they are.

What are "Life Resources"?

Life resources are materials, money, and **other assets** necessary for efficient living.

Many of us are familiar with the understanding that capital is monetary or material in nature. In industries their assets would also include staff.

I'd like us to go beyond the corporate sector and begin to identify the **"other assets"** that are crucial to our advancement concerning destiny.

First, I want to share this story with you.

After high school, I major in Criminal Justice because I wanted to make a difference in how the law administered Justice.

A noble thought, right?

At least I thought so.

However, my turning point came when my professor asked the class if they could defend a client that was guilty of harming a child.

One-by-one, I could hear my colleagues give an unequivocal Yes!

Then, it was my turn to answer.

Apprehensively, I said, "NO! My conscious won't allow me to." Defending the guilty would have been difficult for me to live with especially with the admission of culpability.

That day, I realized I was pursuing the wrong vocation.

At some point, I started thinking about owning my own business, and that spark grew into desire and changed my trajectory.

I began taking accounting and management courses as I understood the importance of being a good steward of my resources.

Besides, if I was going to own my own business and needed to hire an accountant, wisdom said, "*You better know what the accountant is doing with your money.*"

The accounting courses gave me the understanding of principles and practices; while management taught me how to manage resources efficiently.

As part of the undergraduate prerequisite for graduation, each student had to complete a capstone project.

The project assignment entailed the development of an Urban Ministry to meet the needs of the community. For me to collect my data, I would have to conduct an ethnographic analysis.

An ethnography study is the systematic study of people and cultures which include a brief history, and an analysis of the terrain, the climate, and the habitat.

Stay with me!

I had to detect the assets within the urban district I was studying.

Keep in mind that the community was an improvised inner-city with several abandoned, dilapidated buildings that were visible blemishes to both residents and visitors.

As I glanced over the area with my spiritual lens, I was fascinated by the countless amounts of resources that were concealed in the community. They have been overlooked and hidden because people could not see the value.

For example:

The children and teens playing outside; the elderly person walking.

The teen sitting at the bus stop; the Transit System.

The playground with the broken swing.

The vacant lot with overgrown trees.

Optimistically, this should cause disruption in your previous frame of reference when distinguishing your own personal assets.

Life Resources can be divided into two groups:

I refer to them as,

1. Tangible/Obvious-assets you can touch.
2. Intangible- these are the assets that are immaterial and cannot be felt with the hand.

Let's look at a few that I noted. The list provided should help you get started when you begin to take inventory of your personal resources.

Tangible Resources

House, Car, Degrees, Finances, Family, Electronics

Intangible Resources

Here's a list of a few examples of tangible assets.

- Mind
- Attitude
- Character
- Dedication
- Passion
- Values
- Conviction
- Gifts
- Principles
- Time
- Commitment
- Faith
- Talents
- Courage

Next, we will look at the benefits of taking full advantage of your resources by allocating them to activities with the highest impact on your outcomes.

Integrate Possessions with Purpose

Here is a simple illustration that explains this concept:

Let's consider the life of a man the United Nations named as the "Messenger of Peace" in 1978.

He dedicated his life to helping people around the world.

He had goals that went beyond furthering his wealth and material possessions.

He was renowned globally as the Champ and one of the Greatest Boxers of all times.

By now, you probably figured out to whom I am referring.

Yes. Muhammad Ali (Cassius Marcellus Clay, Jr.)

How the "Greatest" lived his life best illustrates getting the most out of your assets.

While Ali had many noticeable assets, his list of intangibles were broad.

However, Ali knew his dominate assets and invested them into competitive boxing to acquire an international platform to achieve his higher purpose of altruism, liberation, and global citizenship.

I noted a few of them to show how Ali maximized his potential by incorporating assets with the aim to accomplish his greater life calling.

Resources	How Ali Capitalized on Them
Positive Mental Attitude	He knew he was going to be the greatest despite adversity and consistently declared it. "I am the greatest; I said that even before I knew I was."
Definiteness of Purpose	He refused movies roles, television and endorsement opportunities unrelated to his call.
Conviction / Sacrifice	He stood for his beliefs with great sacrifice and was convicted, imprisoned, stripped of his title, wealth, and popularity.
Courage/Perseverance	He returned to the ring and reclaimed his title.
Faith/Dedication	He kept his mind on his higher purpose
Benevolent	He believed that money was a tool to fulfill philanthropic efforts and gave millions to many causes.
Discipline/Time	He spent years of training and hard work to master the skill of competitive boxing, "I hated every minute of training, but I said, 'Don't quit. Suffer now and live the rest of your life as a champion.'"
Boxing	He noted that boxing was the vehicle he used to introduce him to the world.

Ali was undeniably one of the greatest fighters of his generation both in and out of the ring.

He attained great success by investing his resources wisely.

How are you investing your possessions?

Are they being used towards your goals and objectives that are part of your higher purpose?

Where are you devoting most of your time?

These questions are asked to merely cause you to evaluate your current spending and investing habits figuratively speaking.

Reflection Moment

Many people are endowed with a plethora of resources. But, everyone is given the same three indispensable resources. Each person is given a mind and an equal amount of time to effectively utilize wisely and to make the best use of them. Lastly, we all are given the freedom of choice.

Consider who, what, when, why, where and how you choose to invest these possessions as this will determine where you will end up in life.

CHAPTER 6

Using the Keys to Success

Success is the sum of all these small things on your destination towards purpose

First and foremost, I want to give you a round of applause for making it this far on our journey. Undoubtedly some of you have been developing your plans while others have delayed the process.

Great Job!

If you have been working through the chapters. This will be an easy reference for you to use.

For those of you that have procrastinated and many of us have been there before, here is an opportunity for you to get started on your road to success. I have summarized it for you to have at your disposal.

If you desire to achieve any level of success, you have been presented with a step-by-step guide in the previous chapters and a streamlined version of the DREAM System in this section.

Do not hesitate to refer to an earlier chapter for more detailed explanations.

I made this as a reference section that you can utilize in the future.

Even though you have the five keys, here is a way to organize them in your mind to give you a better understanding of the implementation.

Let me suggest these keys that will help you with the application.

Here are three areas and a way for you to remember it. These are the ones I have chosen to highlight.

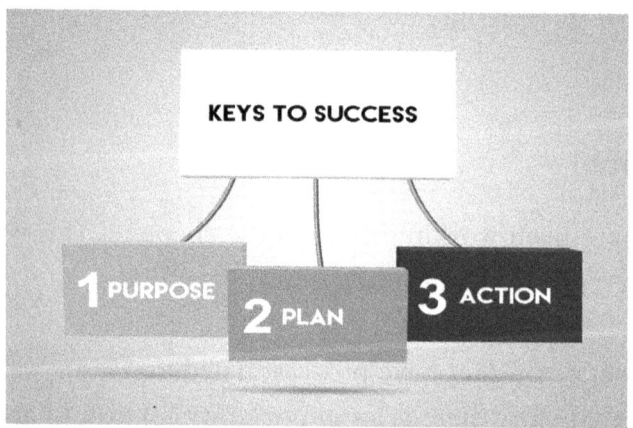

The demand of definiteness of purpose and the ability to visualize the end before the beginning.

Phase I: PURPOSE

1. Discover your "IKIGAI" Reason for Being[2] by employing these practices:

Four steps to finding your purpose

a. Prayer & Meditation- Ask God to reveal Your Purpose

b. Focus on your deepest, most inner longings. They are the voice of your spirit, calling you to the precise place where you belong. Write them down.

c. Make a list of the following:

- Current and Past Vocation, Education,
- Volunteer Work,
- Religious Activities,
- Unique Skills,
- Hobbies and other things you enjoy doing.

d. Write a list of all the traits (intangible resources) you possess (e.g. Adventurous, Helpful, Encouraging).

Look for overlapping themes. You can also use your LinkedIn profile if it is all-inclusive. This will give a snapshot of the life that wants to live through you.

2. Clarify your purpose by asking is this solely for the betterment of myself or others.

Four guiding principles to help clarify your purpose

a. Does your mission/ assignment line up with your Values/ Faith/Belief/System?

b. Will your purpose benefit others? Remember, what you were born to do is for others. God will never give you an assignment just to make you wealthy.

c. It will require your dependency on a Power greater than yourself and other people.

d. Does it pass the SMEL Test? (Spiritual, Moral, Ethical & Legal).

---

[2] *https://en.wikipedia.org/wiki/Ikigai accessed 12/14/2016.*

Phase II: PLANNING

1. Apply proper planning to ensure that you are putting action and feet to manifesting your dreams, goals, and objectives.

Use a Strategic Planning Model to assist in the process

SMART

S – Specific (or Significant).

M – Measurable (or Meaningful).

A – Attainable (or Action-Oriented).

R – Relevant (or Rewarding).

T – Time-bound (or Trackable).

VIPER

V – Visualize: Truly imagine the goal.

I – Implement: Implement methods to succeed in the goal.

P – Planning: Distinguish plan factors based on techniques.

E – Execution: Get moving on the plan and goal.

R – Recap: Evaluate the outcome and future steps.

2. Relentlessly pursue and prioritize proper goals that are unique to achieving your objectives (Trello & Kanban)(www.Trello.com)

3. Persevere as you face the landmines detours and early exits you will encounter on your journey towards a destination. Eliminate both the physical and mental distractions that come to take you off course and impede progress as discussed in Chapter 3.

4. To circumvent preventable complications and capriciousness, do not overlook planning in these areas in the illustration below.

The Work-Life Balance

Again, it is imperative that you devote proper care and maintenance in these key areas of life to stay balanced.

USING THE KEYS TO SUCCESS

Phase III: ACTION

1. Take Inventory of the possession that is stored in your treasure chest and is waiting to be opened and used to accomplish your purpose

2. Proper Management of your resources to maximize them to get the most value or best return on their asset.

3. Know that in time you will reap a return on your investments.

4. Be a blessing to others by giving.

Now, here you have the tools that will get you there. Once you have managed all these, you will discover the rewards are truly promising.

Here is to your dream life.

Best to your success on your endeavors as you continue to move towards achieving the Life, Relationships, and Business Success You Imagined and Deserve.

Final Note

The last assignment that I would like to give you is something that has helped me immensely. As I mentioned earlier, journaling is an important part of discovering your purpose. Therefore, I am providing you a 31-day journal so you can document your journey towards success. This will get you started before you purchase a stand-alone journal.

The D.R.E.A.M SYSTEM JOURNAL

DAY 1

The D.R.E.A.M SYSTEM JOURNAL

DAY 2

The D.R.E.A.M SYSTEM JOURNAL

DAY 3

The D.R.E.A.M SYSTEM JOURNAL

DAY 4

The D.R.E.A.M SYSTEM JOURNAL

DAY 5

The D.R.E.A.M SYSTEM JOURNAL

DAY 6

USING THE KEYS TO SUCCESS

The D.R.E.A.M SYSTEM JOURNAL

DAY 7

The D.R.E.A.M SYSTEM JOURNAL
DAY 8

USING THE KEYS TO SUCCESS

The D.R.E.A.M SYSTEM JOURNAL
DAY 9

The D.R.E.A.M SYSTEM JOURNAL

DAY 10

The D.R.E.A.M SYSTEM JOURNAL

DAY 11

The D.R.E.A.M SYSTEM JOURNAL

DAY 12

USING THE KEYS TO SUCCESS

The D.R.E.A.M SYSTEM JOURNAL
DAY 13

The D.R.E.A.M SYSTEM JOURNAL
DAY 14

The D.R.E.A.M SYSTEM JOURNAL

DAY 15

The D.R.E.A.M SYSTEM JOURNAL
DAY 16

The D.R.E.A.M SYSTEM JOURNAL

DAY 17

The D.R.E.A.M SYSTEM JOURNAL
DAY 18

USING THE KEYS TO SUCCESS

The D.R.E.A.M SYSTEM JOURNAL
DAY 19

The D.R.E.A.M SYSTEM JOURNAL

DAY 20

USING THE KEYS TO SUCCESS

The D.R.E.A.M SYSTEM JOURNAL
DAY 21

The D.R.E.A.M SYSTEM JOURNAL

DAY 22

The D.R.E.A.M SYSTEM JOURNAL
DAY 23

The D.R.E.A.M SYSTEM JOURNAL
DAY 24

USING THE KEYS TO SUCCESS

The D.R.E.A.M SYSTEM JOURNAL
DAY 25

The D.R.E.A.M SYSTEM JOURNAL
DAY 26

The D.R.E.A.M SYSTEM JOURNAL
DAY 27

The D.R.E.A.M SYSTEM JOURNAL

DAY 28

USING THE KEYS TO SUCCESS

The D.R.E.A.M SYSTEM JOURNAL

DAY 29

The D.R.E.A.M SYSTEM JOURNAL

DAY 30

The D.R.E.A.M SYSTEM JOURNAL
DAY 31

About the Author

Dr. Carla McArthur is a Transformational Life Coach specializ-ing in helping women deal with the overwhelming prospect of "loss and life-shifts" in their personal and professional lives. By helping her clients unlock their inner-self, they can achieve the balanced, healthy, and purposeful life they desire.

Before starting her coaching practice, Dr. McArthur devoted two decades to providing leadership to nonprofit and faith-based organizations where she used her gifts of counseling, coaching and mentoring individuals and families. She has been a fierce proponent of women and youth empowerment and has dedicated herself to not only coaching clients but also educating them about the issues affecting their quality of life.

Dr. McArthur holds a Doctor of Ministry in Christian Counseling and a Master of Divinity with a concentration in Psychology of Religion in Pastoral Counseling. She also completed graduate studies in Nonprofit Management. She is a Licensed and Ordained Minister, NCCA Licensed Pastoral Counselor, Certified Tempera-ment Counselor, and Nationally Certified Entrepreneur Coach.

She enjoys, traveling, working out, the fine arts; and most of all, Laughing-out-Loud.

Dr. McArthur is available for motivational and transformational seminars, speaking engagements and workshops. She can be contacted at (470)-207-1936 or *drcmcarthur@gmail.com*. For more information please visit: www.carlamcarthur.com

Resources

Organizes your projects into boards *www.Trello.com*

Task Management Tool *www.wunderlist.com*

Understand How You Spend Your Time *www.rescuetime.com*

www.ingramcontent.com/pod-product-compliance
Lightning Source LLC
Chambersburg PA
CBHW070124100426
42744CB00010B/1910